EVERYDAY
PROPHETIC

A CLEAR WITNESS

RUTH
HENDRICKSON

Everyday Prophetic – A Clear Witness
by Ruth Hendrickson

Unless otherwise noted, all Scripture quotations are taken from the Holy Bible, New Living Translation (NLT), copyright © 1996, 2004, 2015 by Tyndale House Foundation. Used by permission of Tyndale House Publishers, Inc., Carol Stream, Illinois 60188. All rights reserved.

Cover Design | Yvonne Parks | PearCreative.ca

To contact the author | www.RuthHendrickson.org

ISBN: 978-1-7354902-2-9

TABLE OF CONTENTS

Then I fell down at his feet to worship him, but he said, "No, don't worship me. I am a servant of God, just like you and your brothers and sisters who testify about their faith in Jesus. Worship only God. For the essence of prophecy is to give a clear witness for Jesus."

—Revelation 19:10

CHARTING THE COURSE

I well remember learning to read maps in school. We had a box of maps and we would be given a starting point and a destination. We had to locate the correct map(s) that would be needed to make the journey, decide what the route would be, and figure out the mileage and the stopping points along the way.

That ability to read maps is a lost art for many today. It is so much easier to just plug in the destination in the GPS system, and our smart phone does all the work. Within the blink of an eye, we have multiple choices for the route and estimated travel time. In fact, they will even correct the route if there is an accident, construction, heavy traffic, or if we happen to make a wrong turn.

Too often I see this "get to our destination as quickly and directly as possible" in terms of the prophetic.

Scripture gives us many examples of the way a prophetic gift is to be used. This includes the simple basics of building each other up and encouraging one another. And it includes many stories of tried-and-true saints that walked in high levels of prophetic gifting and some who held the office of prophet.

However, one thing I see today is that many people try to just plug in the destination of prophet without taking time to study. I would suggest that there is an invitation from God to slow down, take the scenic route with Him, and learn along the way. Learn to hear His voice and to test His words. Take time to develop a healthy culture in which the prophetic can thrive and where people can grow. Learn to take personal responsibility for the wrong words that you may speak, and to be humble and give God the glory for the right words that you do speak. In some ways, we have become so focused on a perceived destination, that we have missed the sights along the way.

My desire is to lay out a road map for you to grow in the prophetic. You can use it on your own, but It is also my hope that churches and bodies of believers will use this material for training. Oh, to see the church walk in the fullness and health with all the gifts of the Holy Spirit.

BUILDING BLOCKS AND POWER TOOLS

How do we develop a culture that builds people up? For whatever reason, many cultures tear people down. Yet, as followers of Jesus Christ, we are created to be Kingdom changers. We are created to have influence far beyond what the world can ask, see, or imagine.

> Let the message about Christ, in all its richness, fill your lives. Teach and counsel each other with all the wisdom he gives. Sing psalms and hymns and spiritual songs to God with thankful hearts. And whatever you do or say, do it as a representative of the Lord Jesus, giving thanks through him to God the Father.[1]

---

1 Colossians 3:16-17

What would happen if the truth about who Jesus Christ is, and who we are in Him, really filled our lives? How would that change what comes out of our mouths? How would that open us up to minister to each other? And even more so, how would that open us up to the prophetic?

This is something that I dream about. For years, I have watched many people tear others down. We think we are seeing and understanding; however, often we are seeing through a distorted lens of our painful experiences, incorrect belief systems, and personal opinions. How often we forget that our vision is flawed.

> Now we see things imperfectly, like puzzling reflections in a mirror, but then we will see everything with perfect clarity. All that I know now is partial and incomplete, but then I will know everything completely, just as God now knows me completely.[2]

It is vital that we be committed to a radical lifestyle that honors God, and therefore, allows us to ultimately see others through His eyes. Using earthly eyesight and understanding will always leave us short of the calling of God. We can only be true encouragers and

---

2   1 Corinthians 13:12

It is vital that we be committed to a radical lifestyle that honors God, and therefore, allows us to ultimately see others through His eyes.

prophetic people when we are looking from Heaven's perspective.

No matter what, you were created to be great, awesome, and mighty in the Kingdom of Heaven! But how does that happen?

I grew up in a traditional church where we often recited the Lord's Prayer.[3] Unfortunately, all I did was recite it. There is a marked difference between reciting something and allowing it to impact our mind, will and emotions. I was doing what I was expected to do and that was all. It was not until many years later that the words in that prayer began to truly impact my life.

What does it mean for God's will to be done on earth as in Heaven? What does it mean for God's Kingdom to be on this earth? Too often we are busy trying to pull earth up to Heaven as we live in our natural mindset, when God has specifically said that

3   See Matthew 6:9-13 and Luke 11:2-4

is not right. We are to pull Heaven's realm onto the earth.

Stop here for a few moments. Let me invite you into a realm where you can dream with God.

It is within our very DNA, as sons and daughters of God, to bring Heaven down to earth. We were created to operate outside the bounds of the possible, and within the realm of the impossible. We were created to not only make disciples of all nations, but also to leave a legacy.

Going Deeper and Taking Ground: Grab Your Journal!

Take a moment and think of the last time you received a word of encouragement. Write that out in a journal.

Think about the last time someone believed in you, when you were not sure you believed in yourself.

Remember the last time you tried to do something that you believed or knew was impossible, in and of yourself. What happens when you remember these situations? Are you encouraged? Excited? Or is there a sense of frustration or even failure?

As you able to allow these encounters and memories to become fuel for your future? Or, have they become a noose around your neck?

Take a moment and dream hand in hand with God. Ask Him to release a dream within you with what it means for His will to be done on Earth as in Heaven. Ask Him what your part in that looks like. Make sure you write down what you see, sense or hear Him saying to you. Do not disregard any impression or any Scripture that He may show you.

If I could speak all the languages of earth and of angels, but didn't love others, I would only be a noisy gong or a clanging cymbal.

— 1 Corinthians 13:1

CREATING ATMOSPHERES

We are challenged to create an atmosphere of encouragement, where growth and change are encouraged and expected.

I remember years ago that I was tasked with making major changes to a ministry. Along with this, I had inherited a team of precious people who had a specific way of doing things. With the changes I would have to implement, they would have some decisions to make. Were they going to embrace growth and change or run from it? As a leader, I had to chart the course and invite them to come along. However, I also realized that I could not force them to make the changes. Since I was new in this role, I agonized over the implementation of the changes. In the midst of that agony, my boss told me to set the new standard for ministry and to set the bar high; to encourage people and to trust them. He went on to say that some would decide the changes were too much, the bar too high, and would naturally leave the ministry, while others would soar.

That is what I did, and it turned out to be great advice. As we transitioned, there was one person who decided that the leap was too great and left the team. The rest wrestled through the changes with me and became stronger, both as individuals and also as a team. The results were amazing.

God has made available to us the tools that are needed to effect change. In addition, He is ready and willing to help us grow in using these tools.

Tools provided by the Kingdom of Heaven are not meant to be kept safely in a toolbox or stored on a shelf. Tools provided by the Kingdom of Heaven are meant to be used in greater ways than we can even imagine.

I guess you could say that every tool that God provides automatically becomes a POWER tool when plugged into Holy Spirit. Now, there is power!

> Tools provided by the Kingdom of Heaven are not meant to be kept safely in a toolbox or stored on a shelf... they are meant to be used in greater ways than we can even imagine.

Spiritual Gifts: Our Power Tools

We would be remiss if we didn't talk about the spiritual gifts and the need for them to be wrapped in love. The church has seen a lot of misuse of both love and the gifts, so we want to lay a firm foundation before we dive further into the prophetic.

In 1 Corinthians 13, Paul speaks directly into what comes out of our mouths. We are reminded that any earthly language and any heavenly language (tongues) is no more than noise if it is not well wrapped in the love of the Father. As we continue to weave through this powerful chapter, we find that the same argument is made for all the spiritual gifts.

Earlier, I related the spiritual gifts to being power tools. Power tools have tremendous potential to do damage when not used correctly. They can tear down and destroy rather than create something beautiful.

However, when anything that aligns with Scripture is wrapped with the love that comes from Heaven, mountains are moved. Let me clarify that God's love will always draw people closer to Him. The love of God will always challenge our earthly mindsets and idols. The love of God does not accept everything, but it does love everyone. The love of God will always draw us to the heart of God.

When we truly manifest the love of Jesus Christ, it will be evident through every area of ministry and invade every area of our lives.

Going Deeper and Taking Ground:
Grab Your Journal!

Earlier in this section I made the following statement: "Tools provided by the Kingdom of Heaven are not meant to be kept safely in a toolbox or stored on a shelf. Tools provided by the Kingdom of Heaven are meant to be used in greater ways than we can even imagine."

What are the tools that you know God has given you?

Now, take a moment and ask Him is there are tools that have been sitting in the shelf. If so, no worries, just ask His forgiveness for not using them and give Him permission to teach you how to use them. He is very faithful!

As they listen, their secret thoughts will be exposed, and they will fall to their knees and worship God, declaring, "God is truly here among you." —1 Corinthians 14:25

IMPACTED WITH POWER?

Many people walk through the doors of the church with some hesitation. There are those who have been greatly wounded within the church, while others have little to no church experience. Of course, many have been affected by those leaders who have fallen into moral failure and made the news headlines, causing former or "would be" faithful to believe that there is no hope. Finally, we have people who have walked through the doors of the church only to feel condemned by well-meaning church members about their faults, sins, and failures.

Both believers and unbelievers need to encounter the Living God when they walk through the door of the church. They need to find a God who is truly God, and not just a historical figure on paper. Believers need

to represent Jesus Christ at a whole new level. We need
to be healed up and shored up ourselves, walking in
our God-given identity and comfortable with who
God created us to be. When the church truly begins
to walk in her identity and in health, what unbelievers encounter when they walk through the doors will
change.

I mentioned earlier about people feeling condemned by well-meaning church members, as their
faults, sins, and failures are pointed out. I have to wonder what would change if, when people walked into
church, or into the presence of a believer, they encoun-
tered their potential and their God-ordained destiny.
What would change?

1 Corinthians 14:25 captivated me with that
thought and I began to dream with God about this
concept.

> As they listen, their secret thoughts will be
> exposed, and they will fall to their knees and
> worship God, declaring, "God is truly here
> among you."[4]

As *who* listens? As the unbelievers listen. Verse 24
tells us that they will be convicted of their sins and

---

4 1 Corinthians 14:25

judged by the prophetic word. Often, we read that and throw the judgment into the prophetic. However, if that is what it was all about, I think they would fall down repenting of their sins. Which is what intrigues me about Verse 25, because they fall down in worship, not repentance.

Let's ponder that a bit more as we realize that they fall down in worship as their secret thoughts are brought forth. I have to wonder, given the wording used here, if what is being exposed, their secret thoughts, are actually the God-given hopes, dreams, promises and purposes that God placed within them. Could it be that with the prophetic they come face to face with who God created them to be, rather than the judgment of their sins? We tend to know our sins, but we don't always know the desires of our hearts. When God begins to show the unbeliever a different picture, their life has the capacity to change in mighty and powerful ways.

> When God begins to show the unbeliever a different picture, their life has the capacity to change in mighty and powerful ways.

Isaiah 45:3 also speaks into this.

"And I will give you treasures hidden in darkness – secret riches. I will do this so you may know that I am the Lord, the God of Israel, the one who calls you by name."[5]

All the gifts of the spirit are meant to be powerful and effective. The prophetic is no exception. As believers, how often do we long for a prophetic word? A heathy prophetic word, given in the God-ordained moment, can change the trajectory of our lives. The same is true for an unbeliever, in fact even more so, as with that word we can introduce them to the King of Kings and Lord of Lords.

With this additional understanding, it is vital that we develop a healthy prophetic culture that goes well beyond the walls of the church. We need to tend to our own issues, bring our churches into health and wholeness aligned with Scripture, and bring the prophetic into our day-to-day lives to truly impact the world with power.

---

5   Isaiah 45:3

Going Deeper and Taking Ground:
Grab Your Journal!

What has your experience of "church" been?

Ask the Lord if there are any judgments or vows that you have made against the Body of Christ. And, if so, this is a great time to confess, repent and break them.

Take some time and dream with the Lord. What would it look like if we truly learned to release Healthy Prophetic words in a God-ordained moment that carried the potential to change the trajectory of a life?

"And why worry about a speck in your friend's eye when you have a log in your own? How can you think of saying to your friend, 'Let me help you get rid of that speck in your eye,' when you can't see past the log in your own eye?"
— Matthew 7:3-4

DEVELOPING CULTURE

Do you have anything in your life that is unhealthy? I think that if we were to take an honest assessment of our lives, we would all discover that we have something to work on!

With that said, we can trust the Holy Spirit to bring up those things, as that type of assessment is best done in conjunction with the Holy Spirit rather than on our own. After all, Psalm 139 reminds us that God searches us, and He also knows us!

"O Lord, you have examined my heart and know everything about me."[6]

Therefore, it is important that we go before the throne of grace, and hand-in-hand with the Lord, we

---

6   Psalm 139:1

look at our habits and evaluate how we are dealing with the "junk" in our lives. We need to take a look at the health of our relationships with other people. It is important that we guard our relationship with the Lord, spending time with Him and growing in intimacy with Him. Finally, if we truly desire to walk in the prophetic, we need to be willing to walk in accountability. Most prophetic people who end up off-track, are not walking in true accountability with other believers and have become lone rangers.

In Matthew, we are reminded that we are not to point out the speck in someone else's eye without dealing with the log in our own eye first.[7] Therefore, we must be aware of our own junk and actively work on it. If we are not doing this, we are more likely to dump our junk on someone else under the guise of prophecy. When that happens, we heap bondage and shame on the individual, rather than healing and freedom.

So, it's time to take off that mask and get real with ourselves and with the Lord. Then we can truly help move others forward into their God-given destiny. Part of the God-ordained destiny for every believer is to be a spiritual father or mother to someone else. So, get rid of that mask – we have work to do!

---

7   See Matthew 7:3

Going Deeper and Taking Ground:
Grab Your Journal!

Is it difficult for you to take off your mask and get real with yourself and the Lord? If so, why?

Sometimes we know what areas in our lives are unhealthy. And at other times, we don't. Ask the Lord to reveal any place (belief or behavior) that does not align with His word. Remember, if He reveals something, it is not for shame; it is for freedom.

Take some time to dream with the Lord. What would it look like if the body of Christ were to walk in healthy vulnerability and transparency? How would that impact what the world sees when they look at the church?

"You have heard me teach things that have been confirmed by many reliable witnesses. Now teach these truths to other trustworthy people who will be able to pass them on to others." – 2 Timothy 2:2

SPIRITUAL PARENTS – SPIRITUAL MENTORS

Parents shelter children when they are younger, but as they get older, they begin to equip them to walk into the world around them. As the children get even older, there comes a time when they leave the safe shelter and we parents have to trust that we have equipped them to navigate the world around them. We have adult children and although they are out and about in the world, we are still here for them. However, in the midst of the various transitions that we walked through with them, we love to see them soar. And we will help them get back up when they fall. That is what parents do in the natural and that is what spiritual parents also must learn to do.

You have been believers so long now that you ought to be teaching others. Instead, you need someone to teach you again the basic things about God's word. You are like babies who need milk and cannot eat solid food. For someone who lives on milk is still an infant and doesn't know how to do what is right."[8]

In the verse above I see a mandate from the Kingdom of Heaven that we have a job to do. We have to grow up and teach others. We must absorb the basic things of God's Word so that we can intake the solid food. We must know our identity and be secure in who we are in Christ so that we can call others into that same place.

Many have grown up without spiritual parents. I believe that this has drastically impacted the health of the church today. Rather than the church being a place where people walk through the doors and come face-to-face with the heart of God, they often meet people who are still trying to figure out who God is themselves.

As we were raising our children, in the natural, we would encourage them and rejoice with them. We also worked to equip them for their future. And there were

8   Hebrews 5:12-13

certain core values that we wanted to see reproduced in them to make them strong as adults.

As with many things that are mirrored in the natural, it is the same in the spiritual. I am going to switch from the term spiritual parents to spiritual mentors as mentor is a word that is better understood today.

A spiritual mentor helps people grow in their identity, giftings, and passions. They help the individual to become well-grounded in the Word of God and in an intimate relationship with God. A spiritual mentor can look at the reality of the moment while looking ahead at a God-ordained future and helping the person make the journey.

For many years I have trained teams to do emotional healing. One thing I have experienced and have seen team members experience is an ability to have God-given vision. The best way to describe it is that we look past where the person is and view their God-intended future. And we look to the Lord for help as they navigate the pathway to healthy and wholeness in God.

Why do I share this in conjunction with the prophetic? Because we have come to a day where the prophetic does more than come into the church and give a word. There is an army of prophetic people buried in the church that have a calling to look at an individual and see beyond the moment. And this is the army that will often walk with the person into their destiny. But to do this we have to learn to see from a different perspective.

Going Deeper and Taking Ground:
Grab Your Journal!

Have you had spiritual mentors in your life? If so, what was the impact? If not, that does not disqualify you from becoming a spiritual mentor to someone else.

Write out Psalm 145:4, 2 Timothy 2:2 and 1 Corinthians 11:1. What do you learn about teaching others in those verses?

Dream with the Lord. What would it look like if the Body of Christ became a prophetic army of people waiting for people to walk through the doors so that they release destiny over the individual?

CAPACITY VS. EXECUTION

Graham Cooke makes a great statement, "Every one of us in the church has the capacity to prophesy. We can be a prophetic statement of what the Kingdom of Heaven is – showing people what Christ is really like – by our lifestyle, our actions, our thoughts, our identity. We're a prophetic voice of who God is, how He speaks, and what He is doing on earth. We cannot help but be prophetic; it is in our very bones. It is who God made us to be."[9]

Step back and read that again, and then read it a third time. If the body of Christ could truly grab hold of what Graham is saying, I imagine that everything

---

9   Graham Cooke, *Approaching the Heart of Prophecy*. Vacaville, Brilliant Book House, LLC, 2006 p.6

would change. Often, we think that no one is watching, but in essence, the world is watching. I am a prophetic voice of who God is and you are a prophetic voice of who God is. It's in our very bones…it's in our DNA!

> *"Salt is good for seasoning. But if it loses its flavor, how do you make it salty again? You must have the qualities of salt among yourselves and live in peace with each other."*[10]

How often do we pick up the salt to flavor our food? The believer brings the flavor of the Kingdom of Heaven to the earthly realm. One of the many ways this happens is through the prophetic voice. Not everyone is a prophet, but every believer has a God-given capacity to prophesy, to be the salt and light of the earth. Knowing that we have the capacity, and acting on it, are two different things. We can intellectually agree that we have the capacity and ability to prophesy. However, if we never allow the words to come out of our mouths, then we can never be salt and light to a hurting world.

> *Open your mouth wide, and I will fill it with good things.*[11]

---

10   Mark 9:50
11   Psalm 81:10

> The believer brings the flavor of the Kingdom of Heaven to the earthly realm. One of the many ways this happens is through the prophetic voice.

I think of this verse often in conjunction with the prophetic. As the only way we can be a prophetic people and create a prophetic culture is if we are willing to open our mouths. Now, of course, as I say this, we also have to understand that the power of both life and death are in the tongue,[12] so our tongue must be conditioned to bring life and not death and destruction.

I have watched many prophetic people lean into the prophetic models that are found in the Old Testament. There are many lessons that we can learn from the Old Testament prophets. However, when these are not seasoned with the power of the Cross, we can quickly bring death and destruction where God has ordained us to bring life and health.

It is not my intention to go into an in-depth study of Old Testament vs. New Testament prophecy in this book. However, let's take a few minutes to point out a few key differences.

---

12   See Proverbs 18:21

In the Old Testament, the Holy Spirit rested on specific people for a specific time period or service. A few examples:

- Jonah – calling for the repentance of Nineveh.
- Watchmen such as Ezekiel – calling out the times and seasons.
- Jeremiah – who we know as the weeping prophet, shed many tears as He spoke the Word of God.
- Elijah – and his famous battle with Baal.

If you want to be an Old Testament prophet, I'd encourage you to think again. They carried a very heavy mandate.

> But any prophet who falsely claims to speak in my name or who speaks in the name of another god must die."[13]

We can never take the call to prophesy lightly. However, at this moment we can be thankful that we live on this side of the Cross of Jesus Christ.

On this side of the Cross, both the one giving the prophetic word and also the one receiving it are called to "test" the word.

---

13   Deuteronomy 18:20

"Dear friends, do not believe everyone who claims to speak by the Spirit. You must test them to see if the spirit they have comes from God. For there are many false prophets in the world."[14]

One of the definitions of the word "test" is basically "a critical examination, observation, or evaluation".[15] In the Old Testament we were told to stone the prophets if they got a word false. However, in the New Testament we are told to test the words.

We have to understand that this does not remove the responsibility from the one giving the prophetic word. It is vital that the prophet still be very careful and weigh the word before it comes out of their mouth. However, it also puts a responsibility on the one that is receiving the prophetic word. Both must understand that it is ultimately up to the receiver to determine if they are going to accept the word. However, even with that understanding, it is the responsibility of both the one giving the word and the one receiving the word to test it. Why? Because Jesus sent the Holy Spirit to all believers. And one of the roles of the Holy Spirit is to be a source of wisdom, revelation, and power.

---

14   1 John 4:1
15   www.merriam-webster.com/dictionary/test Accessed 4/10/2020

"But it was to us that God revealed these things by His Spirit. For His Spirit searches out everything and shows us God's deep secrets. No one can know a person's thoughts except that person's own spirit, and no one can know God's thoughts except God's own Spirit."[16]

The other component that we have is asking other mature believers to also weigh the word. We also find this piece of advice in 1 Corinthians.

Let two or three people prophesy, and let the others evaluate what is said.[17]

That verse also takes us right back to the need for accountability and walking with others. And we are not to get uncomfortable or degrade prophetic words as they come forth, nor should we shut them down. Doing so is in direct conflict with Scripture. We cannot pick and choose the spiritual gifts that we are going to allow. It's all or none. So many people argue that the prophetic brings a mess within the church. I do believe that Paul was very aware of this. In 1 Thessalonians He reminds us:

"Do not stifle the Holy Spirit."

---

16   1 Corinthians 2:10-11
17   1 Corinthians 14:29

When I look up the word stifle,[18] it means"

- To quell, crush, or end by force
- To suppress, curb, or withhold
- To kill be impeding respiration; smother
- To suffer from difficulty in breathing, as in a close atmosphere
- To become stifled or suffocated

There are a number of times throughout Scripture where we see Holy Spirit described as wind.[19] In other words, we are to allow the Holy Spirit to be that wind and we are not to suppress, curb or even withhold the move of God through the prophetic word. I am not saying that there should not be protocol and order. I am saying that Holy Spirit must be allowed to flow through all the gifts.

> We are to allow the Holy Spirit to be that wind and we are not to suppress, curb or even withhold the move of God through the prophetic word.

---

18 www.dictionary.com/browse/stifle?s=t. Accessed 4/10/2020
19   For example see Acts 2:2; John 3:8; John 20:22

In addition, we are told, "*Do not scoff at prophecies.*"[20] A more common word for scoff may be the word mock. We are not to make fun of or mock the prophetic word. So, not only do we have to allow it, we also have to be open to receive the prophetic word.

Finally, Paul reminds us to "*test everything and hold on to what is good.*"[21] Again, we see that word to "test." I would also suggest that if we are told to test, then there will be times when the entire word or portions of the word are not correct. And, since we are told to hold on to what it good, then there also must be words that we are to let go of and not hold onto.

---

20   1 Thessalonians 5:20
21   1 Thessalonians 5:21

CRUCIAL KEYS

*"One of the most important things to do in a
church that wants to nurture and administrate
the prophetic ministry, is to dial down the
mysticism with the desire to look super
spiritual."[22]*

Although the above quote refers specifically to
corporate gatherings and the manner in which
churches handle the prophetic, I believe that this
same concept carries over to the individual. Over the
years I have met many well-meaning, albeit strange
prophetic people. In fact, some are so strange, they
are scary.

---

22   Mike Bickle. *Growing in the Prophetic.* Lake Mary. Charisma
      House 1996, 2008. P. 105-106

I don't believe that God meant for the prophetic to push people away. In fact, remember that, "As they listen, their secret thoughts will be exposed, and they will fall to their knees and worship God, declaring, "God is truly here among you."[23] Since this verse is talking specifically about unbelievers, I see them being drawn in by the prophetic, not running away. In addition, they fall to their knees and worship. There is no strange mysticism; there is only the power of the prophetic word fueled by the Holy Spirit.

In 2012 I attended a school of the prophets at Bethel church in Redding, California. As Kris Vallotton was sharing, he made a powerful statement.

> "The primary purpose of prophecy is not to direct or correct the body of Christ, but rather to encourage the church. We should never allow people who are ministering in the gift of prophecy to speak negatively into the lives of others. The goal of the gift of prophecy is to bring out the best in people! We are to mine the gold that is among the dirt and to find the hidden treasures in the lives of people."

---

23   1 Corinthians 14:25

"The goal of the gift of prophecy is to bring out the best in people! We are to mine the gold that is among the dirt and to find the hidden treasures in the lives of people."

– Kris Valloton

This really spoke to me. Over the years I had seen, heard and experienced the prophetic being used as a hammer of correction, rather than to represent the heart and passion of the Lord for a person. Public prophetic words brought a lot of condemnation, rather than healing and freedom. There is a place for that difficult word of correction but that should be the exception and not the rule. Rick Joyner puts it this way:

"The prophetic heart is one that is in union with God's heart. Prophetic eyes are eyes that see what He sees. Therefore, the goal of all prophetic ministry should be to be in union with Him."[24]

---

24 Rick Joyner, *The Prophetic Ministry*. Fort Mill, MorningStar Publications Inc. 2009 p.145

— KEYS: —

- A prophetic word is not a guarantee of what is to come to pass.
- A prophetic word is a catalyst for change or an invitation to step into something with God.
- A prophetic word requires our active participation to come to pass.

Many people have received a prophetic word, thinking that it is a guarantee. However, God always invites us into the process. Therefore, the prophetic word is not a guarantee but an invitation.

Sometimes the prophetic word serves as fuel or a catalyst. We may have a hidden desire, placed within our very being by God. As the word is received, we find our spirit soars and that word acts as fuel to propel us forward with that situation.

— KEY: —

- Every prophetic word also has a timing component with it.

Many people have walked away from a prophetic word, not because the word was wrong, but because their timing was wrong. When we receive a prophetic word, we must step back and ask God about the timing. It may be a now word or it may be a later word. Stepping into a later word in the now moment can actually abort the prophetic word and the reverse is true also.

— KEY: —

- **We cannot look inward for the prophetic word; we must look upward.**

I well remember a woman coming up to me for prayer. I asked her what she would like prayer for, and she responded that I was the prophet, so she wasn't going to tell me. In and of myself, I cannot give a prophetic word. It is dangerous to even attempt to make something up. Don't allow the pressure to perform to impact your ability to minister. God never gave me anything for that woman, so I didn't prophesy over her. She was so unimpressed! Never compromise to please man (or woman). Always look to please God.

— KEY: —

- **The method or ministry style that we use can never produce the word.**

How often do we look for the latest and greatest formula for ministry? I suspect that we are all responsible for doing this at some point. We can scream and shout, and even put on our best King James voice. However, if it is not God, then what impact does it truly have except to make us look crazy?

Think about this. It is very possible that God will release a prophetic word to you to give to someone just because of who you are. He made you unique and wonderful – so although the word must come from Heavenly realms, the presentation is likely to have a bit of you mixed in.

With that said, we do use models and methods as we teach. They are tools that we use to equip the saints. We can be confident that as we are learning, God will use us powerfully even with using a model/method. However, as we grow in our gifting, we move away from the specific model and become more comfortable in flowing with Holy Spirit.

— KEY: —

- **Alignment is vital!**

Every prophetic word that we give (or receive) must align with the whole of Scripture. There are no exceptions to this. In addition, the prophetic word must align with the heart and nature of God.

2 Timothy 3:16 is a powerful reminder of the value of Scripture.

"All Scripture is inspired by God and is useful to teach us what is true and to make us realize what is wrong in our lives. It corrects us when we are wrong and teaches us to do what is right."[25]

Paul took this concept very seriously. In Galatians 1 he talks about truth being twisted and contorted in such a way that people actually turn away from God. In verses 8-10 he begins a discourse which really shows his conviction:

"Let God's curse fall on anyone, including us or even an angel from heaven, who preaches a different kind of Good News than the one we preached to you. I say again, what we have said before: If anyone preaches any other Good News than the one you welcomed, let that person be cursed. Obviously, I'm not trying to win the approval of people, but of God. If pleasing people were my goal, I would not be Christ's servant."[26]

---

25   2 Timothy 3:16
26   Galatians 1:8-10

Bishop Bill Hamon makes a powerful statement, "Abuse happens when there is an 'elevation of prophecy' to the same level of authority and inspiration as the written Word of God, causing cultic groups who esteem prophetic utterance as Scripture."[27]

We must fully understand and embrace the fact that Scripture is complete and sufficient, and resist the temptation to elevate the prophetic word, or any other word, to the same level. At the same time, we must remember that we have a personal responsibility to test everything we hear, back to the Word of God. This does not just apply to prophetic words but also to everything we read, every sermon that we listen to, and anything else that comes at us. The Scripture is a plumb line that can be trusted.

— KEY: —

- **Do not allow and/or do not give secret prophetic words.**

One of the other situations we have seen develop is people attempting to give secret prophetic words. One of the wonderful things about walking with Jesus is that God brings light. I strongly discourage people

---

27 Bill Hamon, *Prophets and the Prophetic Movement.* Shippensburg. Destiny Image Publishers 1990

from giving/receiving prophetic words in secret.

People who use prophecy to flatter and manipulate others often seek to prophesy in secret so that others do not see what is happening. They desire to isolate the person they are prophesying to so that others will not tip them off as to how foolish and underhanded this type of prophecy is.

Mike Bickle gives powerful insight into this situation: "These people prophesy out of their own desires to motivate people to connect with them. They will use flattery and exaggeration to meet the desires of other people and then gain an upper hand over them."[28]

Bill Hamon, when talking about church prophetic ministry, states: "The prophetic ministry has the power to either bless or curse, so all words must be witnessed to and judged by those who are spiritually mature and are in oversight in the local assembly".[29]

When I prophesy over people, I encourage them to have someone else with them and also, they are free, and encouraged, to record it. Recording actually becomes a safety net for both of us as we can "hear" or "remember" incorrectly, so it gives a record. In addition, it allows them to listen to it over and over. It allows

---

28 Mike Bickle. *Growing in the Prophetic*
29 Bill Hamon. *Prophets and the Prophetic Movement.* p 137

them to test it back to Scripture at a different level rather than trying to do it from memory. Finally, listening to a correct word over and over, allows it to sink into the very core and become ingrained or solidified in us.

Those who walk in the light do not mind giving prophetic words in the light. They do not mind being held accountable for those words. And a healthy prophetic voice will be willing to acknowledge and take ownership when they give a wrong word.

Proverbs 18:21 talks about life and death being in the power of the tongue. We usually relate this verse to gossip, which is good. However, I also want to pull it into the prophetic. We are always responsible for what comes out of our mouths. End of story.

Satan would love to steal away the prophetic words that God speaks over our lives. We need to be aware of that and shut those doors. We cannot afford to "forget" the word God speaks or to mis-interpret the authentic word of God.

> *"But one who prophesies is helping others grow in the Lord, encouraging and comforting them."*[30]

---

30 1 Corinthians 14:3

— KEY: —

- **Be very cautious and careful with giving or receiving words into domestic areas.**

When we talk about domestic areas, we are talking about areas such as: Marriage/spouse, babies, financial investments, moving, financial decisions, school/college to attend, etc.

With these areas, Godly counsel is wise and welcome. However, when it crosses over into the prophetic realm, it can create great disappointment and confusion.

I know of an individual, who as a young teenager, received a prophetic word that they already knew their spouse. That word actually held them "captive" for years as they struggled to come to grips with it. The person(s) giving the word were highly respected and carried a lot of spiritual authority in the individual's eyes. However, eventually this opened the door for a very unhealthy relationship with someone within their realm of relationships. Could the word have been true? Sure, it may well have been true. Even so, remember there is also a timing component and it also could have been wrong. Wisdom would have withheld the word rather than releasing it.

Another challenging area is having children. This is an area where we must tread carefully. We must be able to fully separate an authentic word from God pertaining to having children from our own desire for the couple. An authentic word from God brings encouragement and will be confirmed by a pregnancy. On the flip side, one from our sympathetic heart/mind will provide a Band-Aid for a moment, but open the door for confusion, disappointment, and disillusionment down the road.

— KEY: —

- **Language is important!**

When you are learning to prophesy, I would suggest that you do not use the language "God said," "God told me" or something similar. When that type of language is used, the individual you are giving the word to has no choice but to accept the word.

However, you can say something along the line of "I am sensing something, may I share it with you?" This type of question allows for conversation afterward. If it makes sense to them, you can always share that you have been learning to use the prophetic gift and that you sensed what you shared with them was from the Lord.

Another way you can engage them is to tell them, "I am learning to walk in the prophetic, would it be okay if I shared with you what I am seeing/sensing?" Again, this allows them to accept or reject the word.

And remember, if the person does not want you to share, that's okay too. Don't take it personally. And please don't try to force it on them.

With all that said, personally I will often just share the word in the context of a general conversation. Because I didn't add in all the "God" language, well-meaning people would tell me that I was not prophetic. However, people would come back all the time talking about the prophetic word I had given them.

Allow God to move in and through you and use you as you!

— KEY: —

- **Don't over-emphasize personal prophecy.**

What do I mean by personal prophecy? Some people feel like they need a word from the Lord to make any type of decision. We have a God-given brain that is to be used. He gave us the ability to reason and make decisions. I believe that when Adam named the animals, he was not asking for a prophetic word, he was just partnering with God in everyday life.

If our ear is tuned to God, we can be rest assured that when we truly need a prophetic word, He will make sure we get one. And the rest of the time, we can trust the wonderful brain that He has given us and the leading of the Holy Spirit.

Remember...

For the Lord is the Spirit, and wherever the Spirit of the Lord is, there is freedom.[31]

— KEY: —

- **The heart of the Father is always to bring freedom.**

Any prophetic word must point to Jesus Christ. In addition, a true prophetic word will always bring an invitation to freedom, not to shame or bondage. Since prophetic words should lead to freedom, never release, or receive a word that carries judgment or criticism with it.

I heard a story of a pastor who released, from a pulpit, a prophetic word that a member of the

---

31   2 Corinthians 3:17

congregation was struggling with pornography. There were a number of problems with this. The first was that he knew that the person struggled with pornography, so it was not a prophetic word at all. The Holy Spirit had not revealed that, so it was illegal to identify what he said as a prophetic word. The second issue is that a true prophetic word will never bring shame. So…even if the pastor had not known the person struggled with pornography in the natural, the word never should have been released as it brought the individual shame and bondage rather than an invitation to freedom.

We have to be aware that people with critical and judgmental spirits will often flock to the prophetic. Needless to say, we need to be aware of this and make sure that we are not falling into that trap. In addition, if we are administrating a prophetic team, we must be willing to address those with critical and judgmental spirits. They need healing before being released to minister in the prophetic.

— KEY: —

- A valid prophetic word will glorify Jesus and exalt God.

There have been many individuals, both well known and unknown, who have released prophetic words that pointed to themselves or to their ministries. A valid prophetic word will always point to Heaven.

Ever since the garden of Eden, humankind has struggled to continually point to God and not to self. And we can struggle not to worship the angels, but to worship God alone.

> *"Then I fell down at his feet to worship him, but he said, 'No, don't worship me. For I am a servant of God, just like you and other brothers and sisters who testify of their faith in Jesus. Worship God. For the essence of prophecy is to give a clear witness for Jesus.'"*[32]

I love that last sentence. "For the essence of prophecy is to give a clear witness for Jesus". Do our prophetic words give a clear witness to our Savior? If they point any other direction, then they are not valid words.

Another way to summarize this is that God's grace is on a prophetic word. That is the grace to give, to receive, and for the word to manifest in His time.

— KEY: —

• Watch your body language and actions.

---

32 Revelation 19:10

People do experience manifestations of the Holy Spirit. These can include things like shaking, laughing and more. The challenge is that many people do not believe that they can or should control these manifestations. However, Paul admonished and required that believers contribute to order within the body by using self-control.

First, we have to have love to be our highest goal. Take a moment to read through 1 Corinthians 14. Look at the push and pull with the gifts. And also his heart for unbelievers. Everything is wrapped up in verse 23:

> Even so, if unbelievers or people who don't understand these things come into your church meeting and hear everyone speaking in an unknown language, they will think you are crazy.[33]

We don't want unbelievers to focus on the crazy, we want them to see the glory and love of the living God.

— KEY: —

- **Be careful how you identify people.**

We want to be very careful when using labels. Labels, in the spiritual realm, have a tremendous sticky value and can be difficult to remove.

---

33 1 Corinthians 14:23

Remember, we are told to test the prophetic words. This tells us immediately that we will be wrong at times. Because someone gives an incorrect prophetic word doesn't necessarily mean that they are a false prophet. It means they are human and are learning and growing. When walking in the prophetic, we must exercise grace and mercy.

Rick Joyner makes a fantastic statement pertaining to false prophets:

> "There is a simple factor that distinguishes false prophets form the genuine ones. False prophets use their gifts and other people for their own ends, in order to build up their own influence or ministry. True prophets use their gifts in a self-sacrificing way, for the love of Christ and the sake of His people. Self-seeking, self-promotion, and self-preservation are the most destructive forces in ministry. Like King Saul, even if we have been anointed by God, we can nevertheless fall into witchcraft if those forces gain control of us."[34]

Words that focus on sin, judgment, condemnation, and hopelessness do not point to the nature of God

---

34   Rock Joyner. *The Prophetic Ministry.* Fort Mill, MorningStar Publications 1977 p 79-80

but can actually tell us a lot about the person who is prophesying.

Furthermore, when we find someone, in our midst, who continually offers incorrect words, points to self, researches information on people to make their word look legitimate, etc., then those in leadership must be willing to take the necessary steps to protect the congregation.

With that said, what do you do if leadership is unwilling to do anything about the individual and their prophetic words? Remember, we don't have to receive everything. We test and make sure the word aligns with the heart, nature and Word of God. If it doesn't align, throw the word out. It's okay, you really do have permission! You are responsible for what you take in. No one can "force" us to receive a prophetic word – false or from the throne room of Heaven. The choice is ours!

— KEY: —

- **If a Prophetic word has timeframes, use tons of caution!**

The other day I got out some steak and decided to put it in a marinade. Had I just dumped the marinade on and immediately grilled it, there would not have been much flavor. However, by allowing the steak to sit in the marinade for a time, the flavor of the marinade mingled with the natural flavor of the steak and created a different flavor. It took the two working together to bring forth the power.

With the prophetic, we need to recognize that God's definition of time and our definition of time are often quite different! How often have we watched God come through at the eleventh hour? I find it interesting that we expect Him to act within our timeframe in the moment.

Let me share some of my personal story as recorded in my book *Positioned*.[35]

"For years, I had a repeated prophetic word over my life. I'd heard the initial word and received a call into ministry while I was at the Toronto Airport Christian Fellowship many years before. As the years went on, I would hear the word again through both well-known prophetic voices and not so well-known prophetic voices. I began to joke that God just had to hit the play button to give me a prophetic word. Little did I know that when Patricia King came on the scene, God hit the play button and the season shifted. In

---

35 Ruth Hendrickson, *Positioned*. 2019

this case, what was once a future word suddenly became a now word."

I share that because that word marinated within me for over a decade before I walked into the "now" moment. Through those years there were many times when I wondered if I had missed God's timing. It would have been so easy to run ahead of God. Peter must have understood this as the Holy Spirit had him write, "But you must not forget this one thing, dear friends: A day is like a thousand years to the Lord, and a thousand years is like a day."36 That Scripture alone should warn us that God tells times and seasons much differently than we do. And it should alert us that we need to be very careful with timeframes buried within prophetic words. As I look back, I realize that had I not recognized that there was a timing component to the prophetic word, I actually would have risked aborting the fullness of that word on my life. Let me share the rest of the story.

> "Looking back, I realize that I was not aim-
> lessly roaming for all those years. God had me
> on a planned journey. We were stopping, study-
> ing, learning, and healing along the way. Yes, I
> even got battered and bruised in the process.

---

36   2 Peter 3:8

However, God was faithful to use that for my good as well. As we journeyed together, God was healing my heart and teaching me to keep a short account of wrongs. He was teaching me to be a leader and increasing my wisdom. He was teaching me to pack differently, that I didn't need all the painful baggage that I was trying to carry. I needed all the tools that He would equip me with. He was teaching me to use new skill sets and providing mentors along the way. He was teaching me to dream with Him, to utter His prophecies, adjusting my identity to align with His, and pulling me out of my comfort zone over and over."

— KEY: —

• We must participate for the Prophetic Word to come to pass.

Many people believe that if they "hear" or are given a prophetic word that it will come to pass automatically and soon. However, God delights in inviting us into the process. Therefore, our participation is required.

You can have a new car sitting in the driveway, however, if you don't get in and start the ignition and put it in gear, it's not going any place. God can give us the prophetic word, but it requires our participation to be accomplished.

We talked about this earlier, however, it bears repeating. In the book of Genesis, chapters 16-21 we find the story of Abraham and Sarah and their struggle to have a child. You may recall that God gave them a word that they would have a child. In their humanness, once they got over the shock of what God was saying, they assumed that the word would come to pass in a specific timeframe. When that didn't happen, they took matters into their own hands and found another way to have a child, as Abraham slept with Sarah's maid. However, this was not God's plan and the impatience and rationale of Abraham and Sarah created a challenge to God's perfect plan that we still feel today.

God, in His mercy, still gave them the promised child. However, it was in His time and His way, not theirs.

In that case they had to wait for His time…but they also had to participate. Sarah did not immaculately conceive their son. Let's just say it took both of them trusting God and acting on what He had promised. Yes, they made a huge mistake – but God is still faithful.

Kris Vallotton puts it this way: "We need to realize that God seldom does things all by Himself. He often requires us to be involved with Him to see our destiny fulfilled. The key here is to allow the Holy Spirit to show us what part He wants us to play and what part God has reserved for Himself. Otherwise, we create Ishmaels who will persecute our Isaacs!"[37]

We must be very careful to look at the prophetic word through Heaven's lenses rather than our own. The fullness of the prophetic word must always belong to God. In a sense, He is inviting us on a journey of exploration with Him, as we learn the components that are contained within the very heartbeat of the word.

Let me state again, it is important to remember that prophetic information about a person or about a situation doesn't automatically come with wisdom, power or even authority to walk into or change a situation. That information only becomes beneficial as we see through Heaven's perspective rather than our own. This is true whether we are on the giving or receiving end of the prophetic word.

---

37   Kris Vallotton. *Basic Training for the Prophetic Ministry.* Shippensburg. Destiny Image Publishers, Inc. 1982. P 60

— KEY: —

- **Make sure you follow the "stop" of the Holy Spirit**

I was talking to a wonderful woman of God. She was energetic and had a very strong prophetic gift. However, as strong as that gift was, there was a stronger barrier to healthy prophetic. She felt that she also had to give an explanation or interpretation of what she felt the prophetic word was. As I challenged her to stop when the Holy Spirit says to stop, she refused. Basically she was unwilling to trust God enough that He would speak to the people and/or use others to bring clarification, if needed.

We must work to hear the voice of the Lord and recognize how He speaks in and through us. We need to be comfortable enough to stop when the Holy Spirit stops, even if it doesn't make sense to us.

Revelation and understanding of the prophetic word will also come in bits and pieces. It is of upmost importance that we understand this, so that we can allow the Holy Spirit lots of room to move.

"Search me, O God, and know my heart; test me and know my anxious thoughts. Point out anything in me that offends you and lead me along the path of everlasting life."

— Psalm 139:23-24

VALUES

As we look to minister prophetically, we need to take a good look at our values. This is a key component in each and every area of our lives, as it becomes the lens through which we see and interpret what we see, and also what we hear.

> "Do not judge others, and you will not be judged. For you will be treated as you treat others. The standard you use in judging is the standard by which you will be judged. And why worry about a speck in your friend's eye when you have a log in your own? How can you think of saying to your friend, 'Let me help you get rid of that speak in your eye,' when you can't see past the log in your own eye?' Hypocrite! First get rid of the log in your own eye; then you will see well enough to deal with the speak in your friend's eye."[38]

---

38 Matthew 7:1-5

When we talk about principles and boundaries, we are talking about personal beliefs and components of our lives that determine our response.

When something happens around us, it will quickly determine what we believe and what we value. When we have boundaries, they determine what we will do and what we will not do. The values that we develop will feed into our desires and what things/people are important within our lives. Finally, all these plus more will dictate how we see God. Is that an important relationship that we are taking time to develop? How much are we willing to trust Him? How much of our lives are we willing to relinquish or yield to God? Ultimately, this all impacts how well we learn the sound of His voice and how we release a prophetic word.

As we grow in the prophetic, we must allow the Lord to continually search our hearts. David, who God calls a man after his own heart,[39] understood this concept.

"Search me, O God, and know my heart; test me and know my anxious thoughts. Point out anything in me that offends you and lead me along the path of everlasting life."[40]

---

39 Acts 13:22
40 Psalm 139:23-24

TREASURE HUNTING

Let's go back to 1 Corinthians 14:24

"But if all of you are prophesying, and unbelievers or people who don't understand these things come into your meeting, they will be convicted of sin and judged by what you say."[41]

This scripture doesn't specifically state if it is referring to an unbeliever or other individual who is actually being prophesied to. Maybe, but then again, maybe not. What we know for sure is that they came into the meeting.

However, as we continue to read, there is a key. *"As they listen, their secret thoughts will be exposed."*[42] It's

---

41   1 Corinthians 14:24
42   1 Corinthians 14:25

almost like God was letting them listen in on a private conversation, giving them a glimpse into the Kingdom of Heaven. As we continue to dive into this verse, it goes on, *"they will fall to their knees and worship God, declaring, 'God is truly here among you.'"* From this verse, we see that the prophetic words have the power to reveal secrets of the unbeliever's heart, as I mentioned earlier. Again, I want to suggest that it is possible that the secret thoughts referred to, may be the hopes, dreams and desires that have been buried deep within the person. They have been buried underneath all the false beliefs, disappointments, and frustrations of life. And we also need to remember that they have a God void in their life that they have been trying to fill with other things.

Imagine being an unbeliever and having your hopes and dreams revealed. As prophetic people, when we go treasure hunting with Holy Spirit, we can end up being the ones God uses to reveal that treasure.

I love the Scripture that talks about Jesus' focus as He faced the cross. In Hebrews, as it talks about keeping our eyes on Jesus, it also tells us that He endured the shame of the cross because of the joy that was set before Him.[43] When Jesus was dying on the cross, do

---

43   See Hebrews 12:2

Imagine being an unbeliever and having your hopes and dreams revealed. As prophetic people, when we go treasure hunting with Holy Spirit, we can end up being the ones God uses to reveal that treasure.

you think that He saw only the sin in our lives, or did he see something that was worth redeeming?

We need to understand that the price Jesus paid on the cross determined the value of the people he purchased. God saw something good in us, even as He knew the full extent of our sin. We need to understand that it doesn't take a prophetic gifting to see sin in both the believer and the unbeliever. However, it does require the eyes of God to see broken people from Heaven's perspective.

When we talk about seeing through God's eyes, through Heaven's perspective, we ultimately are looking to bridge the gap between where they are at this moment and God's intended future.

"But the one who prophesies, strengthens others, encourages them, and comforts them."[44]

---

44   1 Corinthians 14:3

When we speak of edification and growth, we must realize that the basis of this is to build up the individual and call them into their God-intended destiny. Ultimately, when we strengthen them and encourage them, we are calling them near to God. After all, Matthew 11:28 invites all those who are weary to come to the Lord. This is the heart of the Father for His creation. And, when we offer comfort, we remind them that God is near. Remember, we have numerous promises in Scripture that God is our comforter. He is near!

Healthy prophecy begins from an attitude of treasure hunting, not junk hunting. We are looking for and asking God to reveal the pearl of great price, within each and every person.

Now, that is exciting! And when we begin to see God giving the prophetic word to help bring people into freedom and into their destiny, our hearts should sing. What a loving God we have.

Going Deeper and Taking Ground:
Grab Your Journal!

Have you ever given a "junk" prophetic word? One that tears down and condemns rather than builds up and leads closer to Jesus? If so, confess, repent and ask the Lord's forgiveness.

Dream with the Lord. What does it look like when the prophetic flows from an attitude of Heavenly treasure hunting rather than junk hunting? Ask Him to give your spiritual sight to see the treasure, no matter who deep it may be buried.

"A house is built by wisdom and becomes strong through good sense. Through knowledge its rooms are filled with all sorts of precious riches and valuables."

— Proverbs 24:3-4

PROPHETS AND PROCESS

As I have both talked to and sat under the teaching of seasoned prophets, I see a common thread and that is that authentic prophets like process.

> *"A house is built by wisdom and becomes strong through good sense. Through knowledge its rooms are filled with all sorts of precious riches and valuables."*[45]

When we follow God's process, it has the capacity to make us rich in who God is. We become more like Him and grow in the gifts and talents that He has given us.

As I shared in a previous section, the process that I went through was invaluable in getting where God has

---

45 Proverbs 24:3-4

called me to walk. Without that process, I never would have become the person that I am today. This relates to who I am as an individual and also how I minister.

There is a natural tendency to focus on the outcome rather than the process. When I gave birth to my children, I would have much preferred to have the baby in my arms without going through childbirth. However, there is a purpose for childbirth. It is part of the process. It is not unusual in religious circles to also talk about birth pains. So, even spiritually we recognize that there is a process. However, the process is seldom easy to walk through.

Moses could not lead the people out of Egypt without having grown up in the palace. He had to have a leader's mindset. However, with that said, he also could not lead the people out of Egypt without having tended sheep in the desert. He had to learn to live in and understand the desert to take the people through. And in the desert is where he heard the call of God.

Interestingly enough, although we will deny it, most Christians believe in magic. We want God to wave the magic wand and make things instantly appear. We get so focused on the outcome that we forget to rejoice in the process. I wish that I had learned to value process years ago. I have a feeling that I would have navigated it much better and with less pain! It is within the realm of the process that people can lose their anointing and stop short of the destiny that God has placed before them.

With the prophetic, if we short circuit any part of the process, we will stop short of becoming the healthy prophetic voice that God has called us to become. This is why I say that all authentic prophets like process. They don't run from it. They are humble and want to learn from God. Accountability is important. They don't walk alone; they walk in the company of others. They realize that all parts of the body are important. And they know that they can even mess up the prophetic word.

With the prophetic, if we short circuit any part of the process, we will stop short of becoming the healthy prophetic voice that God has called us to become.

Going Deeper and Taking Ground:
Grab Your Journal!

Are you a lone ranger or a team player?

How do you honestly feel about accountability?

These are both vital questions that we need to ask Holy Spirit to shine His light on. We must be part of a Heavenly team in order to carry the fullness of glory that God has. In addition, we need one another. Proverbs 17:17 reminds us that iron sharpens iron! We need each other.

Ask the Lord if there is any area where you have looked to Him as the magic solution rather than the Heavenly solution. If so, take time to confess, repent and ask for His forgiveness.

Take some time and ask the Lord what He wants you to know about Godly process. Why is it so necessary?

If you really want to go deep, study about David or Joseph, intentionally looking at the process they went through.

DARN – FELL INTO A TRAP!

Every believer should value integrity. This value should run through every area of our lives, including the prophetic. And every prophetic word should point the person toward a deeper relationship with God, not draw them away.

Wrong Word...

We have a slew of well-meaning prophetic voices who have been wrong in the word they gave. We owe those around us the truth. When we are willing to admit that we were wrong, that we spoke out of our own understanding, or that we just don't understand, we actually build trust with those who are watching and listening.

When we give an incorrect word and don't address the "mess" but just move on to the next work, we actually sow a seed of distrust. As this pattern continues, we will eventually lose credibility both with believers and unbelievers.

Humility is key to walking in the prophetic. James 4:10 reminds us to humble ourselves before the Lord and He will lift us up. I believe that growing in humility is one of the fastest ways to grow in a prophetic gifting. When I see "pride" tied into the prophetic, it will also give me a caution. However, when I see humility, I also see God's grace.

Going Deeper and Taking Ground: Grab Your Journal!

If we want to become healthy in the prophetic we need to deal with the times we have given a bad prophetic word. In addition, we need to deal with the times we have been given a bad prophetic word. Spend some time with the Lord and work through both of these situations (if applicable). God will take you deeper than you ever imagined. He is just that good!

COMPLEX OR SIMPLE

Another trap that people fall into is believing that they need to give a profound prophetic word. This becomes a snare that can lead the person to "add" to the word or even to make up a word to give. Sometimes competition enters in and the problems just multiply. The prophetic word that we give must align with the heart of God, and sometimes that is the simple word. Simple words can carry more weight in spiritual realms than complex words.

One of the things I love to do with conferences is to have a banqueting table. The teaching centers around the heart of God and His extravagant love. . On the table itself are numerous items that are meant to minister into the hearts of the attendees. In order to prepare the table we spend time with the Lord asking what items are to be on the table and purchase as Holy Spirit directs. We have learned not to question or try to understand some of the simple things that come to mind. Holy Spirit knows exactly what is needed and we can trust Him.

One year our intercessors sensed that we were to purchase a pineapple. It seemed like a rather strange item to put on the table. However, our commitment was to follow the Holy Spirit's leading, so a pineapple landed on the table. As the attendees went up to the table, one person came back hugging the pineapple with tears streaming down their cheeks. There had been a private conversation between them and God. None of us knew about this conversation, yet the Holy Spirit did. That pineapple ministered to her in ways that we could not imagine. With that said remember, sometimes we are called to do a prophetic act rather than release a prophetic word.

One of the most common open doors for this trap is comparing yourself to someone else. Especially when it is the big-name prophet who receives all the recognition and accolades. We must recognize that being prophetic is not about the personal recognition and fame. It's about releasing the heart of God. When we find ourselves looking for the title, it should be a warning that our heart and focus have become unbalanced.

We must recognize that being prophetic is not about the personal recognition and fame. It's about releasing the heart of God.

Going Deeper and Taking Ground:

Grab Your Journal!

We all fall into a trap where we compare ourselves to others. Sometimes this creates growth; however, more often it will stifle that which God has called us to do. You are a unique creation by the King of Kings and Lord of Lords!

Ask the Lord to reveal to you any place or any time where you have fallen into the trap of comparison that has stifled you. Ask His forgiveness.

Ask the Lord to give you a vision of who He created YOU to be. Dream with Him a bit about what that looks like. You can even create a vision board with pictures of some of the things that He shows you.

*"So don't go to war without wise guidance;
victory depends on having many advisers."*

—*Proverbs 24:6*

JUDGMENT!

Throughout the history of the prophetic movement on this side of the Cross, there has been a huge learning curve. Sometimes we try to "justify" the judgmental prophetic word by diving back into the Old Testament. There is so much that we can learn from studying Old Testament prophecy. However, I want to warn you. In the Old Testament it was unthinkable that the prophet could even give a word that was a mix of accurate God-given information and inaccurate information. And it was so unthinkable that the punishment was death.

Within the Old Testament, we see many words and even prophetic actions that have to do with judgment.

If you sense a word of judgment, I take it to those in authority over you, those you are accountable to. Allow the wisdom of Godly men and women to weigh it with you before you risk releasing it. The book of Proverbs has a number of verses that pertain to receiving counsel. One that immediately comes to mind is:

> *"So don't go to war without wise guidance; victory depends on having many advisers."*[46]

Granted, the verse is talking about war. However, note the victory depends on having advisers. As I am learning to grow in the prophetic, I want people walking with me who will call me deeper into the things of God. These same people need to be brave enough to let me know if I am off-balance with the prophetic, or if a word is not to be released. This begs the question, "Am I willing to risk trusting those that God has put beside me to help me grow?"

Many people have been wounded by judgmental words disguised as a prophetic word. Those words usually do not bring life and freedom but rather bondage and shame.

---

46   Proverbs 24:6

The first major trap is that we see something we don't like in the natural and speak a judgmental word to the person. We forget to weigh or even try to season the word with the love of God. Let me ask you a question. Do you want judgment "prophesied" over you? That question usually settles the issue.

The second major trap is when we hear something from the Holy Spirit that can come forth as judgment, and we don't have the maturity or training to know that we don't always speak the first thing that the Holy Spirit shows us. If a word even seems judgmental, we need to step back and ask the Lord what the word of life is that should be released.

Going Deeper and Taking Ground: Grab Your Journal!

This is a great time just to step into the Lord's presence and spend time with Him. Worship and then get quiet before Him and ask Him to speak. Record what you see, sense or hear.

"Open your mouth wide, and I will fill it with good things." – Psalm 81:10

PULLING IT ALL TOGETHER

I hope now you are decreeing and declaring that you ARE a prophetic voice. You don't have to be a big name, have a huge platform, or call yourself a prophet. However, you do have to begin to speak what the Lord gives you.

There comes a point in our walk with the Lord where we have to become intentional. We need to take what He gives us and use it. In fact, we have a promise and a warning in Scripture pertaining to this very concept.

"To those who listen to my teaching, more understanding will be given, and they will have an abundance of knowledge. But for those who are not listening, even what little understanding they have will be taken away from them."[47]

47 Matthew 13:12

When God puts something "in our hands" we need to use it. When that something is a prophetic word, we must learn to release it. If we allow ourselves to be silenced, our voice will be stripped away.

Are you willing to be someone who speaks into other's lives? Not because you are a prophet, but because you are a citizen of Heaven and speak Heaven's language.

If so, pray this prayer and let the Lord know.

Heavenly Father, I ask Your forgiveness for the times when I have not used what is in my hand. I ask Your forgiveness for the times I have kept my mouth shut when You have given me something to share with someone else. And, since You have forgiven me, I choose to forgive myself also.

I thank You that You have created me in Your image. It amazes me that You trust me to speak from a Kingdom perspective. All through Scripture I see people who were willing to radically walk with You. They were people of impact. When I walk with You, I am assured that when I open my mouth that You WILL fill it.[48]

Heavenly Father, I ask for Your heart to love the people around me and to be an instrument that calls others into their God-ordained destiny.

48 See Psalm 81:10

ACTIVATIONS

Remember, you don't have to be a prophet to release a prophetic word. That is what this little book has been about. As I have trained people in the prophetic, I have realized that having some simple exercises can help build faith and confidence. I encourage you to take time to do these. Don't wimp out. Do it with a courage and boldness because you ARE a prophetic voice and you carry the very Kingdom of Heaven.

Letter from Jesus...

This one is for you!

- Put on worship music and worship for 15-30 minutes.
- Grab your journal and a pencil.

- Ask the Lord to write a letter to you.
- Listen and write down what you see, sense or hear.
- Caution: Do not discount what you see, sense or hear. Allow Him to speak.
- Test: As with everything, test it back to the Bible. Does it align with the Word of God and the nature of God?

Encouragement – Family

- Put on worship music and worship for 15-30 minutes.
- Grab a notecard.
- Ask the Lord how He sees each individual member of your family.
  o Alternate: Ask the Lord for a word for each member of your family.
- Write out what you see, sense, or hear on the notecard.

  o Remember, it should edify and build-up. This is not the time for correction or rebuke.

- Caution: Do not discount what you see, sense or hear. Allow Him to speak.

- Test: As with everything, test it back to the Bible. Does it align with the Word of God and the nature of God?
- Leave the note where they can find it.
- Do not expect feedback. The purpose is to bless them. Some may say something, and others will not. Allow that to be okay.

Encourage – Friends

- Put on worship music and worship for 15-30 minutes.
- Grab a notecard.
- Ask the Lord to highlight someone who could use a word of encouragement.
- Ask the Lord for a word of encouragement for that individual.
- Write out the note.
- Caution: Do not discount what you see, sense or hear. Allow Him to speak.
- Test: As with everything, test it back to the Bible. Does it align with the Word of God and the nature of God?
- Mail the note.
- Do not expect feedback. The purpose is to bless them. Some may say something, and others will not. Allow that to be okay.

Encouragement: Phone call

- Put on worship music and worship for 15-30 minutes.
- Ask the Lord to highlight someone who could use a word of encouragement.
- Ask the Lord for a word of encouragement for that individual.
- Make some notes about what you see, sense, or feel the Lord is showing you.
- Caution: Do not discount what you see, sense, or hear. Allow Him to speak.
- Test: As with everything, test it back to the Bible. Does it align with the Word of God and the nature of God?
- Pick up the phone and give them a call. Share what you sense the Lord is saying.

Encouragement: Stranger

- As you are out and about, ask the Lord to highlight someone to you.
- Take a moment and ask Him what He has for them.
- Remember, this may be very simple – it does not have to be long. Do not discount. The

simplest word can have an impact with power when it comes from the Throne Room of Heaven.

- Test: As with everything, test it back to the Bible. Does it align with the Word of God and the nature of God?
- Ask them if you can share something with them and go for it.

These are just a few exercises to get you started. As you grow in hearing the voice of God, you will become more comfortable. You will find that you hear and discern faster. Your faith and confidence will increase.

At some point you will fail; we all do! But that does not give you a reason to stop. It is always an invitation to ask the Lord where we went wrong. Maybe we inserted our own understanding into it or maybe we didn't stop when God said to stop. And honestly, sometimes we just don't hear correctly. Whatever you do, do not allow the doubt, fear or even the demonic to steal your voice.

The prophetic is to be an everyday part of our lives. You are created to be a prophetic voice to the world around you that releases the Kingdom of Heaven!

RUTH HENDRICKSON MINISTRIES RESOURCES

POSITIONED
BOOK AND WORKBOOK

Positioned takes you on a journey where you encounter the God of the impossible through the struggles and triumphs of people just like you and me. You will be challenged and encouraged to tackle every hindrance holding you back so that you can walk in your divine destiny.

This book will show you how to see yourself through God's viewpoint so you can embrace what He is preparing for you.

Available on Amazon and Ministry Website

COURSES AVAILABLE THROUGH MINISTRY WEBSITE

Mashah – Emotional Healing and Deliverance (Basic and Advanced) – A belief-based model for inner/emotional healing and deliverance. Mashah Ministry Training is developed for an individual and team to learn how to minister effectively and safely to see others walking in the healing, freedom, and purity of God.

Ministry Team Training – Designed to bring a "team" concept to the body of Christ. As you walk through this course you'll be provided with a basic framework for ministry that can be used both within the organized church and within your God-given sphere of influence. You'll study Scripture and be challenged to step out, hanging on to Holy Spirit to minister in power. This course has been taken by new believers and seasoned believers, by pastors and laity and it can be taken by you! You can do this!

These courses along with teachings on topics such as anger, shame and forgiveness can be found by visiting ruthhendrickson.org

PERSONAL MINISTRY

If you would like to receive Emotional Healing and Deliverance visit ruthhendrickson.org for cost, application and details.

PERSONAL NOTES

PERSONAL NOTES

PERSONAL NOTES

PERSONAL NOTES

PERSONAL NOTES

Made in USA - Kendallville, IN
1208110_9781735490229
12.08.2020 0822